# How to Manage Your Money

# An Easy-to-Use Guide from the Experts!

## Robert C. Kline

Copyright © 2012 by Robert C. Kline.

All rights reserved. Without limiting the rights under copyright reserved above, no part of this publication may be reproduced, stored in or introduced into a retrieval system, or transmitted, in any form or by any means (electronic, mechanical, photocopying, recording or otherwise), without the prior written permission of both the copyright owner and the above publisher of this book.

This publication is designed to provide accurate and authoritative information in regard to the subject matter covered. It is sold with the understanding that the publisher is not engaged in rendering legal, accounting, or other professional service. If legal advice or other expert assistance is required, the services of a competent professional person should be sought.— *From a Declaration of Principles Jointly Adopted by a Committee of the American Bar Association and a Committee of Publishers and Associations.*

Printed in the United States of America.

**ISBN 978-1-105-63046-0**

# TABLE OF CONTENTS

**CHAPTER ONE**            5
MONEY: WHAT IS IT?

**CHAPTER TWO**            15
INFLATION: WHAT IS IT?

> *How does inflation happen?*
> *Interest rates and fractional reserve banking*
> *Real consumer protection*
> *Another source of inflation*
> *Too little money*
> *Paper money and gold standard*
> *Economic policy and God's law*
> *The real world impact of inflation*
> *What is the cure for inflation?*

**CHAPTER THREE**          35
SEVEN RULES FOR MAKING AND
    KEEPING WEALTH

**CHAPTER FOUR**           41
RULE#7: YOU MUST HAVE A
    FINANCIAL PLAN

> *A word about having faith in yourself*
> *Press on*

**CHAPTER FIVE**        47
*YOU MUST SAVE*

    *The 10% solution*
    *The wonder of compounding interest*

**CHAPTER SIX**        57
*RULE#2: YOU MUST HAVE A BUDGET*

**CHAPTER SEVEN**      77
*BANKRUPTCY*

**CHAPTER EIGHT**      81
*BUDGET FORMS*

**BIBLIOGRAPHY**       91

**ABOUT THE AUTHOR**    93

# CHAPTER ONE

## *MONEY: WHAT IS IT?*

> *"Money is an invention of civilized man in order to be a medium of exchange and raise man from an economic system of barter to a more profitable, advanced and sophisticated division of labor where everyone benefits more."* -- Inflation as an Issue, Dan Brown, II, Shroud Booklet, 1972, p. 3.

The above definition does not really define what money is. Rather, it defines money in terms of what it will do (i.e., its functions). Money's first function is to be a *medium of exchange*. Besides being a medium of exchange, it is also:

- ❖ The standard unit in which prices and debts are expressed.

- ❖ A store of value or a way of holding one's personal wealth.

- ❖ A standard of deferred (or future) payments, such as savings laid by for one's retirement age or emergency.

Of course, in an era of extreme inflation or deflation, money also serves **(very poorly)** as a way of holding one's personal wealth **(store of value)** or as a way of laying by for one's retirement age **(deferred payments)**.

Money as a *medium of exchange* means that *money*, instead of *something else,* is the tool or instrument used to barter or trade goods and services. Strictly speaking, money as a medium of exchange need not have any value beyond that -- being a medium of exchange.

There are two broad views of money held today. The first view holds that money must have *intrinsic value* to be accepted as money, and because it has intrinsic value it is most desired as a commodity. The supporters of this viewpoint reinforce the *metallic standard* – that is, that paper should be based upon a precious metal such as gold or silver, and freely capable of being converted into that metal. According to this standard, the availability of that metal limits the supply of paper money.

The second view holds that money is purely conventional, that by its very nature it has no value as a commodity but is merely a "token" and a "symbol." Those who hold this view say that the substance of which money is made or backed by is irrelevant; that money derives its value from the quantity in circulation in relation to the *quantity* of transactions effected (volume of trade) and its *velocity* (the number of times it turns over in a year). This view is expressed by Irving Fisher in his book, *The Purchasing Power of Money* (New York, 1920), pp. 31-32.

There is a third view which endeavors to combine the other two views. It holds that money must possess both intrinsic value (be converted into metal) *and* derive additional value from its use. This view is best represented by *The Value of Money,* Benjamin M. Andrews, Jr. (New York, 1926), p. 153.

Before money was introduced to mankind as a convenience factor, trade in primitive cultures took place by simply bartering one thing for another. For instance, men exchanged such things as apples for nuts, or cattle for bushels of wheat. But this was very inconvenient and soon became a hassle because of what economists like to call "a double coincidence of wants." That is, it would be an unusual coincidence to always find someone with the tastes or wants that are exactly opposite one's own tastes or wants, or vice versa. So the use of money does simplify things while at the same time raising the level of economic life, because the use of money makes it possible to sell one good for money and then to use the money to buy the goods you wish.

After the Age of Barter but before the Age of Paper Money there was the Age of Commodity Money. Historically, at various times and in various places and cultures, a great variety of *commodities* (goods) served as a medium of exchange:

- Cattle
- Leather
- Hides
- Tobacco

- Copper
- Honey
- Sesame seeds
- Oil
- Wine
- Beer
- Iron
- Gold
- Silver
- Rings
- Diamonds
- Wampum beads (Native Americans)
- Shells
- Huge rocks and landmarks
- Cigarettes (ask any World War II veteran about this)

The list could go on and on. Naturally each of the above has some advantages and disadvantages or they wouldn't have been used as a medium of exchange. However, it is very obvious that cattle are not divisible into small change, the way money can be divided into dollars, half-dollars, quarters, dimes, nickels, and pennies.

Remember, our opening definition of money states that money – especially paper money – makes for "a more profitable, advanced and sophisticated division of labor where everyone benefits more." The key expression here is *"division of labor,"* another favorite expression of the economists.

The three most important features of a modern economic society are:

- Capital
- Division of Labor
- Money

Eventually, the Age of Commodity Money gave way to the Age of Paper Money – our current era. At first, paper money was backed by something that had intrinsic value, like gold or silver. *"Under the gold standard, legal tender was gold or its equivalent in gold-backed certificate issued by the government."* However, paper money today is not convertible into anything that has intrinsic value. The only intrinsic value it might have is that while it is not desirable for its own sake, it is desirable because of the things that it will buy that have intrinsic value. It will buy the things that have always been the main means of holding wealth, such as:

- Land and buildings
- Livestock
- Grain
- Oil
- Wine
- Fine clothing
- Jewels
- Precious metals

However, modern currencies can only have value – that is, can only *buy things* – independent of any gold, silver, or government backing if it is kept in limited supply. An excessive issue of paper money (not converted into gold or silver) will lead to the debasement of that currency and to the rise of prices, or *inflation* (a subject discussed in depth in the next chapter).

Other measures that lead to debasement of paper money are:

- *Excessive borrowing by the individual* **(unlimited credit)** from the banking system for non-productive things.

- *Excessive borrowing by the government* through Treasury Bills and other short-term obligations, which act as near substitutes for money. This, in turn, allows the government to print more money. Both processes lead to an expansion of the money supply and to its consequent dilution **(or *debasement*)**.

All American money today, both paper and coin, is essentially "fiat" money. That is, money is money -- the *medium of exchange* -- because the government has decreed it is so and because we have accepted it as so.

Paul A Samuelson, in *Economics,* Fifth Edition, p. 51, explains what is meant by the expression of *division of labor*: "Men learn that, rather than have everyone do everything in a mediocre way, it is better for fat men to do the fishing, lean men to do the hunting, and smart men to make the medicine, with each exchanging his product for the goods he needs."

*Cattle* have a place of special importance in early economics. The English word *pecuniary* (relating to money) is derived from *pecunia*, Latin for money which, in turn, comes from *pecus,* or cattle, from which also come the terms *capital* and *chattel.*

# CHAPTER TWO

## *INFLATION: WHAT IS IT?*

One key aspect of managing your money is *keeping the money you make*. And one of the major challenges to doing that is *inflation*.

What is inflation? The authors of *Don't Bank on It!* define inflation as, "the condition or state of generally rising average prices for like or equivalent goods or services." To put it even more simply, inflation can be defined as "the uncontrolled process of prices for goods and services constantly rising, while the quality and quantity of the product or service remains constant." This can apply to everything and anything, from a piece of gum to a taxi ride to a haircut that costs "x" amount on January 1$^{st}$ … and "x times 2" just a few months later. That's *inflation*.

Why should you care? Because inflation acts upon

your assets in the same way that erosion acts upon a sand dune, gradually eating away at the size and purchasing power of your nest egg until nothing at all remains . . . unless you work to stop inflation, or at least slow it down.

Inflation is not the first thing most people think of when making long-term plans, and that's understandable. We are taught that money is *money,* and a dollar is a dollar. But that is not so. Money is a fluctuating thing; its *value* – what a given quantity of money can buy – is in a state of constant flux. What money can buy *today* is not the same as what it can buy *tomorrow.*

Consider your paycheck. If you get a pay increase, you naturally assume that your paycheck will now buy more goods and services than it did before the increase. But when you look at it more carefully, you see that your money may actually be buying nothing more than it used to; in fact, it may be buying a bit *less.*

What happened? In this example, the *rate of inflation*

has exceeded the *rate of new income*. That's inflation at its worst, and it personally hurts. By this insidious process, a dollar spent ten years from now may buy no more than what 50 cents buys today.

Of course the *rate of inflation* is not constant either. In the 1980's, the U.S. Department of Labor (the branch of government charged with measuring inflation on a continuing basis) reported that the Consumer Price Index or, CPI, reached as high as 12.4% annually. But as the first decade of the new century drew to a close, the Department of Labor reported that the CPI was approximately 2.1% (and has been trending upward fairly steadily since 2009). At certain points in the recent past – notably the 1980's – inflation was considered a major economic issue in the U.S.; more recently, it has been seen as relatively under control, though economists keep a sharp eye on the indices all the time; they are well aware that a sharp spike in inflation can wipe out savings and drastically alter retirement plans.

The sad fact is that the prices of equivalent goods and services are almost always on the rise. There have been points in history where those prices have actually gone *down* (an event called *deflation*), but they are not common and are often devastating to the economy. An out-of-control rate of valuation in either direction is dangerous.

## *QUESTION: HOW DOES INFLATION HAPPEN?*

## *ONE ANSWER: THE MONEY SUPPLY!*

One major influence on the rate of inflation is *the money supply* – that is, quite simply, how many dollars are available in the economy to be spent on those precious goods and services, from essentials to luxuries. When the overall economy is growing slowly, when unemployment is high, and when individual consumers and families have relatively few dollars to spend, inflation is usually well under control . . . but that is precisely the time when the government, in an attempt to stimulate the economy and create more jobs, may actually inject *more* money into the economy to get things moving again. This process risks inflation.

The money supply can be significantly influenced by the availability of credit, too, giving consumers the opportunity to spend money they haven't made yet. Here, too, more money 'chasing' the same amount of goods and services can increase prices – that is, generate inflation – even when there is no significant increase in employment, salaries, or gross national product. A super-abundance of unsecured consumer credit fueled inflation and created a 'false boom' in the U.S. economy in the years just before and after the turn of the century. Much of that availability came to an end with the financial crises of 2008, which put a (temporary) brake on the inflationary spiral. But things are changing, and will continue to do so. The government-backed bail-outs and 'stimulus packages' of 2008 and 2009 increased the money supply in the U.S. by as much as 15%, and even months later the long-term effects on inflation have yet to be seen. As the authors of an insightful book on the economy, *Aftershock,* have noted, *"Normally it takes about 6 to 18 months for an increase in the money supply to create inflation, but many factors can affect the timing."*

# Real Consumer Protection: The Urgent Need for Tax Reform

*Money, what is it?* "The rise in prices for goods and services isn't necessarily related to an increase in the money supply or available credit. Taxes can inflate the cost of living as well. According to an article from the Tax Foundation that appeared in Grit some years ago, "U.S. taxpayers are earning larger dollar amounts than ever before, but are ending up with less after-tax real income. Median family income has more than doubled since 1970, rising by 105%, [while] direct federal income taxes have risen somewhat faster – 110% in that period." So taxes, both real and "hidden," can take a significant bite out of every worker's salary.

W. Bruce Thomas, Executive Vice President, Accounting and Finance for U.S. Steel, said it well in a recent article in U.S. News and World Report: "The United States needs a modern tax system that will encourage jobs. The need for this reform in our tax laws is critical – and urgent – if our country is to have the new plants and equipment that will restore the strength of America's manufacturing base and provide the growth in meaningful jobs that American workers need and deserve."

# ANOTHER CAUSE OF INFLATION: INTEREST RATES AND "FRACTIONAL RESERVE BANKING"

Interest rates that banks charge on loans, or any form of credit you may employ to buy something, can make the cost of that item skyrocket. It is painfully obvious when a consumer signs a multi-year or high-interest loan agreement and sees the total amount to be paid for the transaction over its term – a figure that is often three or four times the actual purchase price. Translated into plainer terms, your present salary paid to you for your work at your present job would buy three or four times more in America if it weren't for those high interest charges.

The banking industry, through the Federal Reserve System, created credit inflation with "fractional reserve banking." Assuming a bank is required to reserve only ten percent of the money received from a depositor, say $100.

This allows them to use the other 90% of that deposit for other purposes – usually as the funds for a loan to a different customer of the bank. And of course, the bank that receives this second deposit – the funded loan – can use 90% of *that* deposit as well, loaning it to a third customer, who deposits the money in a third bank account . . . and so on and so on. As Gary North points out in *An Introduction to Christian Economics*, "This process continues, until a grand total of $900 comes into circulation from the original $100 deposit." Yet another fast track to inflation, for obvious reasons: a huge increase in the money supply with no increase in goods or services.

# ANOTHER SOURCE OF INFLATION: UNMARKETABLE GOODS

Here is one common, basic mathematical principle that applies to inflation: *The price level of goods and services is equal to the money supply (the amount of money in the hands of buyers) divided by the marketable goods and services.*

Seems simple enough . . . but the word *marketable* is important. You can produce all the *un*marketable goods you want . . . and they don't figure into the equation. By definition, people won't buy *unmarketable goods*. They are not in 'demand' so the law of 'supply and demand' simply doesn't apply. That's why things like publicly funded make work projects habitually fail at stabilizing or growing the economy.

Let's use this example. Say the government pays a million people to produce a million sets of horsehair underwear. Say the government pays each worker a hundred dollars a piece to make each set. That will inject *one hundred million dollars* – an impressive sum! – into the economy, right into the hands of one million people. But face it: *no one* is going to buy horsehair underwear. These products are, almost by definition, *unmarketable*. So they do not truly represent one hundred million dollars in goods, also injected into the economy. In fact, those horsehair underwears represent *zero dollars* in goods injected into the economy, no matter how much the workers who made them were paid.

The net effect? The government has succeeded in increasing the *money supply* in the hands of consumers *without* increasing the goods and services that anyone will buy. That means a hundred million more dollars 'chasing' the same amount of buyable items . . . which means prices will go up. Why? Remember: when you divide the number of *marketable* goods or services (which excludes the horsehair underwear) by the money supply (which is now increased by a hundred million), you have increased the price level index. And in this case, the guy who sells the nice, soft cotton underwear is now going to have a million more people ready to buy his stuff. The law of supply and demand takes over: the supply remains the same; the demand is greater, and prices go up. *Voila:* inflation.

## TOO LITTLE MONEY CAN BE A PROBLEM, TOO

Something else, even more subtle, can cause a rise in the price of goods and services: a limited supply of money – but not in the hands of the consumers, in this case. Too little money (or credit) available to the *producers* of those marketable goods and services can force prices up as well.

When investment money or business loans become too hard to get or too expensive (i.e., if the interest rates are extremely high), money is denied to businesses -- money that could increase production. This causes the businesses with in-demand items to raise prices, since it's the only way they can finance their own growth. This being the case, the "tight money" policies of the Federal Reserve System are actually inflationary instead of anti-inflationary as claimed. And a banking industry that intentionally keeps money scarce -- in order to loan it out with more favorable terms in interest, and horde the assets for themselves – is fueling inflation as well.

# Paper Money and the Gold Standard

There is little doubt that the biggest cause of inflation is the unlimited supply of fiat, or printing press money.

Nobel Prize-winning economist Milton Friedman said, "Inflation is always and everywhere a monetary phenomenon, meaning it can only be created by a central bank, such as the Federal Reserve. True inflation occurs when the Fed increases the money supply at a faster rate than the economy needs it." (Aftershock, page 85)

Gary North, Ph.D., who received his degree from the University of California in economic history and who follows the lead of Ludwig Mises and Murray Rothbard in economic theory, believes that the only safe and sound economy is one where a country's paper money is backed by either gold or silver specifics. In his book, An Introduction to Christian Economics, he points out that gold has functioned historically as money because it possesses the four basic properties that all monetary commodities must have: **durability** (It is impervious to rust or decay), **transportability**, **divisibility** (in its pure state it can be cut with a knife), and **scarcity**.

*Silver is another such commodity that possesses these same four qualities, but because it is in greater supply, its value has generally been less than gold.*

*It is extremely important that money be relatively scarce if it isn't to lose its value as money. Why? Because when governments increase the quantity of money in circulation, or if governmentally licensed and protected banks do the same, the value of the monetary unit will fall and prices go up (or fail to drop, as they would have had the new money not been injected into the system).*

*Why is it that our unbacked printing press money continues to be accepted by the citizenry as though it were backed by gold and silver? No doubt it is because today's paper money looks just like the previous paper money that was backed by gold or silver. But without this restraint of gold or silver, the state can and will continue to print paper money, inflating the money supply in order to keep the boom times going and interest rates low, until the monetary system is destroyed.*

"We would not need gold if, and only if, we would be guaranteed that government or the banks would not tamper with the supply of money in order to gain their own short-run benefits.

As long as that temptation exists, gold (or silver or platinum) will alone serve as a protection against the policies of mass inflation," North said, "The problem is that no substitute to 'full employment' inflationary policies is taboo. What is needed, we are told, is something 'as good as gold,' yet permits domestic inflation."

# *THE REAL WORLD IMPACT OF INFLATION*

Why is inflation – and protecting your assets from it – so important? Because inflation hurts nearly everybody.

- ❖ **Inflation hurts those who are looking for jobs.** An inflated price structure removes the dollars from the economy – dollars that would activate idle industrial capacity and hire the unemployed (or at least those who want to work).

- ❖ **Inflation hurts those who want to retire.** In his famous classic, *The Rich and the Super Rich,* Ferdinand Luneberg quotes statistics that show at least 70% of all Americans are technically poor, in that they have little money saved up or clear title to any personal possessions. Inflation strips a man of any surplus money beyond the minimum costs of survival, destroys savings, and makes planning for a secure retirement perilous and often impossible.

❖ **Inflation hurts those on fixed incomes.** People on fixed salaries that do not keep rising with the cost of living are constantly under threat, along with those depending on fixed-money contracts such as life insurance beneficiaries and annuitants, retired persons living off pensions, landlords with long-term leases, bondholders and other creditors, and those holding cash.

❖ **Inflation hurts businesses**. Business calculations and projections can be distorted so that profits are overstated, thereby allowing the businessman to consume capital that he should be using to increase assets and investments. How is this so? Because of inflated figures on the books, the business owner is not allowed access to enough capital to replace an asset that wears out, and that asset itself is more expensive as well. It will cost much more to have it replaced than it originally cost. Similarly, stockholders and real estate owners may spend part of their capital gains without realizing that they are actually consuming some of their original capital.

- **Inflation penalizes efficient firms and rewards inefficient firms.** There is less consumer resistance to a price increase that occurs in the form of downgrading the quality of a good or service than there is to a price increase tacked onto an existing, unchanging product – even if the product is of high quality.

- **Inflation penalizes thrift and encourages debt.** Why should anyone save money at a certain percent when prices are rising faster than this, resulting in a negative rate of return on savings?

## WHAT IS THE CURE FOR INFLATION? IS THERE ANY?

Thomas Sowell, former professor of Economics at UCLA and a senior fellow at the Hoover Institution in Stanford, California, wrote an article entitled *"Inflation: The Bill for our Illusions."* The piece, which appeared in the *Wall Street Journal* and was sponsored by the SmithKline Corporation, said: *"Inflation isn't baffling at all. To make it disappear, all we need is the political will. The government always seems to be fighting inflation, but inflation always seems to be winning. Is the problem just too complex as we keep hearing? 'Complex' is one of those modern political words. When you don't want to do something, you don't' just come right out and refuse to do it. You say it is 'complex.' Inflation can be licked, but it will take political will to do it."*

# CHAPTER THREE

## *SEVEN RULES FOR MAKING AND KEEPING WEALTH*

These rules are also referred to as "The Seven Cures for a Lean Purse." They come from the booklet, *The Richest Man in Babylon*. The principles of getting and keeping wealth are the same today as they were when Babylon maintained undisputed supremacy as the wealthiest treasure house of the civilized world.

The secret of getting and keeping wealth still applies to the average citizen today, no matter what your job or profession, no matter how much or how little money you have.

Here are the seven rules for getting and keeping wealth:

> 1. *For each ten coins I put in, to spend but nine.*

You must begin at once to start saving at least one-tenth of your earnings.

> 2. *Budget thy expenses that thou mayest have coins to pay for necessities, to pay for thy enjoyments and to gratify thy worthwhile desires without spending more than nine-tenths of thy earnings.*

You must begin at once to budget your expenses and live on nine-tenth of your earnings.

> 3. *Put each coin to laboring, that it may reproduce its kind, even in the flocks of the field, and help bring to the income a stream*

*of wealth that shall flow constantly into thy purse.*

You must begin to invest a portion of the money you have so as to double or triple your savings.

*4. Guard thy treasure from loss by investing only where thy principle is safe, where it may be reclaimed if desirable, and where thou wilt not fail to collect a fair rental.*

You must have sound investments, and for this you must seek out sound money management and counsel.

*5. Own thy own home.*

You must own real estate.

*6. Provide in advance for the needs of the growing age and the protection of thy family.*

You must prepare now for your retirement, while your earning power is high, as well as for the welfare of your dependents. This includes the areas of estate planning (buying insurance, tax shelters, making a will, etc.).

7. *Cultivate thy own power to study and become wiser, to become more skillful, therefore to act as to respect thyself. Thereby shalt thou acquire confidence in thyself to achieve thy carefully considered desires.*

You must set financial goals and establish financial plans to achieve them. You must believe in yourself and have a desire to succeed.

These, then, are the seven steps to financial independence. They are rules that must be carefully followed if one is to get and keep wealth. This is especially true in our day, but it has ever been thus:

- **Arkady of Babylon** started out with only a great desire to succeed, but by wise counsel, careful planning, and shrewd management of his financial resources, he was able to rise above poverty and even realize a surplus.

- **King Solomon**, so the Bible tells us, prayed for wisdom, and the Lord not only gave him great wisdom and understanding about many things, but great riches and honor as well.

- **Jesus Christ**, in the Parable of the Talents, commended the servant who was given five talents and gained five more (doubling his money) and the servant who had two talents and gained two more (also doubling his money), but the servant who had one talent and who would not even put his one talent in the bank so that it could at least earn interest (he buried it instead) was rebuked by Jesus as being most unwise (Matthew 25).

If money was important way back then, nearly three thousand years ago and two thousand years ago, just think how crucial it has become for a happy, healthy, and worry-free life today.

# CHAPTER FOUR

## *RULE #7: YOU MUST HAVE A FINANCIAL PLAN*

Did you realize that *not* having a financial plan could mean the difference between financial success and failure?

Picture a long room with doors at each end. There are many things in this room: money, attractive persons of the opposite sex, books that tell you the secret of happiness and wealth, and many other valuable articles. But also in this room are bottomless pits, traps, hostile persons, dangerous beasts chained in various places around the room . . .

If you had a choice, would you choose to:

1. Go through the room blindfolded, or

2. Go through the room with your eyes wide open and with written instructions on which places and people to visit or avoid.

Of course, all of us would pick the second option. And managing our financial affairs over a lifetime requires the same decision. Isn't it ridiculous, then, that we choose to manage our financial affairs any differently? Ignorance is no virtue, and now we don't have to be ignorant any longer. Now we can manage our financial affairs with our eyes wide open! The means provided is this easy-to-use guide, *How To Manage Your Money*. The written instructions or map that we will use to guide us through our financial maze is the financial plan laid out for us in the Seven Rules for Making and Keeping Wealth.

Remember the Seventh Rule that says, ***"Cultivate thy own power to study and become wiser, to become more skillful, therefore to act as to respect thyself. Thereby shalt thou acquire confidence in thyself to*** *achieve thy carefully considered desires."* Mark it down: you will not succeed financially unless you establish financial goals, have a financial plan to achieve them, and possess the desire or determination to stick to that financial plan. This Money Guide is a no-nonsense guide to help you set those financial goals, establish financial plans, and encourage you to stick to your plan.

It is a well-known axiom that the more income you have, the greater will be your desires, so make up your mind that you will faithfully stick to your plan. Make your financial goal to organize and manage your financial affairs according to the Seven Rules for Making and Keeping Wealth, and let these rules constitute your financial plan for achieving financial success.

## *A WORD ABOUT HAVING FAITH IN YOURSELF:*

Throughout history, the biggest enemy of success

for an individual has been himself. Your biggest roadblock to financial success will be you. You will beat yourself. There are a number of ways that you beat yourself, but the biggest one will be lack of self-confidence. If you are already beat in your head before you start, failure is inevitable. So a most important rule is: **Create self-confidence in yourself. You must believe in yourself.**

Jesus Christ came teaching the ways of God's government and the spiritual laws (ways) of that government. He said, *"Seek ye first the kingdom of God and his righteousness and all these things (material needs) shall be added unto you."* (Matthew 6:33) Both the Old and the New Testaments teach that a man must not make money his god instead of God, but having once learned to live uprightly before God, it was then the will of God to make those who followed God prosperous on this earth.

As a prosperous or wealthy man, we can do more good than as a poor man wandering around and wondering where he will sleep or eat next. Christ said, "Love your neighbor as yourself." In other words, do not hate or punish yourself, actually love yourself. However, love your fellow man as yourself. You want good for yourself, also want good for your fellow man.

"But if much money would corrupt you, so you would no longer care about God, justice, or truth, then better for you to be poor, as you are too weak in character before the temptations of this earth. A poor man who cares about his fellow man can do more good than a rich man who does not care to help his fellow man." (*The Dawn of a New Age for Mankind Through This Economic Association* by Dan Brown, II)

Finally, you must have a desire to succeed. Persevere! Lack of persistence is the reason why most people never even get to first base with respect to financial independence or wealth. Memorize the following proverb and put it into practice in your everyday financial affairs:

# PRESS ON

*"Nothing in the world can take the place of persistence. Talent will not: Nothing is more common than unsuccessful men with talent. Genius will not: Unrewarded genius is almost a proverb. Education will not: The world is full of educated derelicts. Persistence and determination alone are omnipotent."*
*(7 Steps To Freedom by Ben Suarez)*

To succeed financially, your goal must be to organize and manage your finances according to a financial plan. The financial plan you will follow are the Seven Rules for Making and Keeping Wealth.

You must believe in yourself, have a desire to succeed, and use all the rules of finance outlined here if you want to *"cure a lean purse."*

# CHAPTER FIVE

## *YOU MUST SAVE!*

Remember Rule Number One of the Seven Rules: **For each ten coins you put in, to spend but nine.** It's simple, it's true, and it's absolutely essential: quit working for everybody but yourself. Start paying yourself *first* instead of *last*. (For the Christian, this can be the tithe, which is 10% of income.)

One of the cornerstones of personal financial management is the creation of a family savings account, generally at a bank, savings and loan, or credit union. How big should your savings account be? Most experts agree an amount equal to *three months of living expenses* should be a matter of high priority.

# *THE 10% SOLUTION*

Even that amount may seem like an impossible goal. But it can be achieved – thousands of families do it every day. So before you pay off another bill or buy another thing, make up your mind to do it by *saving one-tenth of all you earn,* each and every payday. Ten percent may not seem like enough, but in fact it can become quite a sizeable sum of money over time, and that is what we are looking at right now: the long view, the benefits that build up slowly over time.

It's all about *discipline* and *consistency,* so make an unbreakable rule to *always* pay yourself first, and make it a simple, straightforward amount like ten percent. The commitment can be truly possible, no matter how much you earn.

For example: let's say you make $50,000 a year, and you are paid twice a month. That means you get gross pay of $1,923 twenty-six times a year. One-tenth of that?

$192. You can use a payroll deduction plan at work, automatic transfers from your checking account, or make individual deposit, but whatever method you use, you should put no less than $192 of that paycheck into savings, each and every time you get one.

It's that simple, and that hard. (And yes, there are always taxes, and sometimes benefits, taken from that paycheck before you see it. Of course you can use your amount to make your ten-percent calculation, or even use a different percentage. But the point remains the same: *consistency*.)

Why a savings account instead of some other investment tool . . . or simply hiding it under your bed?

1. Savings accounts are safe, if placed in a financially sound institution. They are automatically insured up to $125,000 by the Federal Deposit Insurance Corporation, a U.S. government agency.

2. Savings accounts are convenient. You can put money in or withdraw it immediately and without penalty.

3. Savings accounts pay interest. The 1% or 2% they currently pay is low, but it's still a lot better than hiding cash under a mattress (remember the unwise servant in the Parable of the Talents!) or doing the banking equivalent: leaving it in your checking account, which pays no interest at all.

The disadvantages of the savings account are:

1. The yield, while good, is not good enough or great.

2. The typical 1% or 2% interest rate on a regular savings account can actually be seen as a *negative* rate of return in an economy that is even moderately inflationary (see the last chapter). If

the rate of return on your savings is 1% or 2% and the CPI is 3% or 4 %, your savings have failed to keep pace, and you are actually losing ground.

## *THE WONDER OF COMPOUNDING INTEREST*

Of course you need immediate access to a fixed amount of money to meet emergency needs, but remember: no one ever got rich from a savings account paying simple interest – that is, interest paid only on the original amount deposited. Therefore, after building your emergency fund, think of investing where you get the greatest rate of return on your money . . . and make sure your savings account *compounds interest daily* (or *continually*). In other words, interest now becomes principal and earns interest.

Not all banks pay the same rate of interest and not

all banks compound interest in the same way. So make sure that your account adds the interest you've earned since the last compounding to your principle balance on a frequent basis – the more frequent the better.

How can you tell? Ask questions like:

❖ What rate of annual interest do you pay? (*Best answer: as high or higher than any other rate you have recently found*).

❖ Do you compound the interest quarterly, daily or continually? (There is very little difference between these last two) (*Best Answer: daily or continually*).

❖ Do you compound from the date of deposit to the date of withdrawal? (*Best answer: date of deposit*).

What's so wonderful about compound interest?

Take a look at these examples: Let's say you deposit $1,000 on January 1, with a compounded interest rate of 5.25%. If interest on that $1,000 is compounded *daily*, and you do nothing else, it will double to $2,000 in slightly less than fourteen years. (The higher the interest rate, the better.) At 6% that $1,000 will double in less than 12 years; at 9% it will double in less than 8 years.) And how long will it take that $1,000 to double at the same 5.25% rate if interest is *not* compounded (what is known as 'simple interest')? 19 years instead of 14 – *five years longer.*

Compound interest is the key to investing and saving in a way that can overcome at least *some* of the effects of inflation. It should be a commonly understood concept and an essential for any savings account, but in fact, people who understand compound interest are rare indeed.

Mr. Baron Rothschild, one of the richest bankers in the world who lived in the 1800's, was asked if he could enumerate the Seven Wonders of the World. He said "No, but I can tell you what the Eighth Wonder should be. The

Eighth Wonder should be utilized by all of us to accomplish what we want. It is *compound interest.*"

**Did you ever stop to think how much money will pass through your hands during your lifetime?**

*Let's assume that you start to work at the age of twenty-five and will be employed fairly regularly until the usual retirement age of sixty-five (or even sixty-seven, now). Let's assume also that your family income will be $50,000 – the estimated median family income for 2010, according to The Trading Report, September 4, 2011. That means that in your lifetime, you will earn the staggering sum of $2,100,000. Even if your yearly income is only half this amount -- $25,000 -- you will earn the impressive sum of $1,050,000. And if you are lucky or smart enough to earn above the median, even a larger amount of money will flow through your hands.*

*Did you ever stop asking yourself, where has all this money gone?*

*That's what financial planning is all about.*

# CHAPTER SIX

## *RULE #2: YOU MUST HAVE A BUDGET*

In broad terms, using money involves:

- ❖ Budgeting
- ❖ Saving and Investing
- ❖ Borrowing
- ❖ Spending

Just what is budgeting? In its simplest terms, it is nothing more than a system (or financial plan) for determining what your personal financial status is at any given time, so that you can determine if you are living within your income or not. Budgets help you determine whether or not you are accomplishing the financial goals you have set for yourself. It also includes breaking down your anticipated income and expenditures into various categories, so you can bring these expenditures under control and keep yourself within the limits of your income. If all works out according to plan, you will have a savings account that you are consistently building up, which is an absolute necessity in order to make financial progress and eventually achieve financial success.

A budget is like a road map. It tells you where you are and how to get from where you are to where you want to be financially – say, five years from now.

## *WHO NEEDS A BUDGET?*

EVERYBODY! Whether it is written down on paper or tucked in the brain. Everybody needs to have their financial affairs under control and managed efficiently and effectively, in order to make the best financial progress and avoid costly financial blunders.

Budgeting enables everyone to plan what to do with

limited resources. Expenses must be brought in line with income, not the other way around.

When you budget, you are investing. You are telling your money where to go instead of wondering where it went.

But budgets don't have to be such a big and complex deal that there is no way they will ever work. Figuring each category down to the exact penny or shifting cash from envelope to envelope usually is self-defeating. Keep your budget "simple." What you should be after is a budget that is effective yet easy to operate – one that doesn't become more of a burden than it is worth. For simplicity's sake, all figures should be rounded off to the nearest dollar.

When should you begin budgeting?

Perhaps you have thought that a person should pay off his debts and then try to save. No, no, a thousand times NO! You are the number one creditor – remember? And the best time to start a budget is NOW.

There are three steps you must take before you actually set up a budget:

1. determine monthly take-home pay from all sources;

2. determine what your monthly **"fixed"** expenses are *"flexible and inflexible";* and

3. determine your monthly bill payments.

We will expand upon these three items as we go.

In this section we have purposely left out ruled budget forms, because if our suspicion is right, you have a natural dislike for them. The idea of filling out a lot of lined-off blank spaces with a detailed account of expenses – *your* expenses – may make you shudder, so we have left them out of this section. However, for the benefit of those few who may want or need ruled-out budget forms, we have included them in the next section, all by themselves. Another form of budgeting is:

## *THE 10-70-20 FORMULA*

This Formula makes provisions for:

- ❖ Savings and Investments
- ❖ Living Expenses
- ❖ Debts

… All at the same time!

This Formula is successful at making you a success with your money because it enables you to do three things:

1. It enables a plan to provide for future prosperity;

2. It enables you to comfortably support yourself and your family; and

3. It provides a way you can pay off your debts.

There are three parts to the 70-20-10 Formula:

## *NEVER ALLOW YOUR LIVING EXPENSES TO EXCEED 70% OF TAKE-HOME INCOME*

Start off by listing your "fixed" expenses on a sheet of paper (or one of our Forms included in the next section of this Money Guide, if you wish). "Fixed" expenses are expenses over which you have little or no control. Do not forget or miss anything; a rather detailed list of items to include can be found in the Forms section that follows this section.

These "fixed" expenses are broken down into "flexible" and "inflexible" expenses. There is a Form for each. Examine "fixed" expenses such as food, clothing, etc., for places to cut back, especially if you find you are consistently spending more than you earn for this category, and you are exceeding 70% of income for these "fixed" expenses. In that case, you are going to have to make some hard choice in terms of where you cut back. Choosing where to cut back is never easy, but it must be done and cannot be avoided if you are going to live within your means and avoid eventual financial disaster.

If your monthly take-home pay from all sources is $4,167 a month, (based on the median income for America of $50,000 a year), you would set aside 70% of take-home pay, or $2,917 ($4,167 x 70%) for "fixed" expenses, which covers both "flexible" and "inflexible" expenses. How much should you spend on each one of those "fixed" expenses? It is impossible to tell. Each person must make up his own budget to fit the individual requirement. The important thing is that you resolve never to allow the total living costs to exceed the 70% of your net take-home pay.

The next part of the Formula is:

## *USE 20% OF YOUR TAKE-HOME INCOME TO PAY DEBTS.*

How much credit should you carry? There are no pat, safe answers or any easy formula to follow. However, most money management experts agree that for the typical middle-class American family it is best if no more than one-fifth (20%) of take-home pay goes for installment purchases or loans. The 20% figure is a suggested guideline, and your family's situation may allow you to exceed that figure. Or the opposite might be true as well; your current situation may require you to stay considerably below 20%. However, in this Money Guide we will stay with the 20% figure for the Formula. (And keep in mind: if you adjust the 20% figure up or down, you will also have to adjust the 70% figure in the formula up or down. And remember, if you do too much adjusting you will adjust away the effectiveness of the Formula.

Paying debts without pain has been a universal problem since Man decided to loan money to his neighbor. It is easier to pay debts than to avoid them. But you must have a Plan, and the Plan must provide that you pay no more than 20% of your take-home pay to rid yourself of your debts (both current and back debts).

Using our monthly take-home figure of $4,167, you would set aside $833 for debts ($4,167 x 20%).

The third and final part of the Formula is:

## *SAVE AND INVEST 10% OF YOUR TAKE-HOME PAY*

Always, with every new paycheck or addition to your income, set aside *at least* 10% for your future estate.

Using that net income of $4,167 per paycheck, the Formula calls for a savings and investment of $417 a month ($4,167 x 10%). Of course, these dollar amounts will change if your income is more or less than the amount used here. For instance, if your yearly income is $25,000 per year, $4,167 becomes $2,084, and $417 become $208. So be sure to work your own family's real income.

If you accept the fact that you are going to live on 10% less of your income – no matter what – and make it an absolute law in your life, a law you will not disobey, you will find that it will not interfere with your standard of living at all.

## *KEEPING TRACK*

What's the best way to plan and track your budget? Start with a simple list – formal or informal.

On a sheet of paper (or using one of our Forms)

make a list of all your debts (or "temporary expenses," as we like to refer to them). As a reminder, mortgage payments do not appear here; they are included with the "Fixed" expenses. After each creditor, list the monthly payment and balance you owe.

For examples, let's say that your list of debts (creditors) looks like this:

## *TABLE ONE*

| Name | Monthly Payment | Balance |
|---|---|---|
| 1. Car payment | $409 | $10,115 |
| 2. Holt's Furniture* | 51 | 5,211 |
| 3. Auto Credit | 51 | 3,065 |
| 4. Electric Appliance* | 158 | 2,146 |
| 5. Small Loans, Inc.* | 112 | 3,065 |
| 6. Federal Bank* | 121 | 6,131 |
| 7. John's Dept. Store | 28 | 920 |
| | **$930** | **$30,653** |

You'll notice that the monthly payment to retire debt in this example is *greater* than the 20% allowed under the "10-70-20" Formula; we are $97 over the monthly allowance of $833. In this case, there are two things you can do.

First, determine what percentages of the entire amount you owe is represented by each individual creditor. In the example, Car payment is 33% of the total debt ($10,115 divided by $30,653); Holt's furniture is 17%; Auto Credit is 10%; Electrical Appliance is 7%; Small Loans is 10%, Federal Bank is 20%; and John's Department Store is 3%. Now take that percentage figure and place it alongside each creditor's name. *(See Table Two.)*

**NOTE:** *This is essentially what is done when you declare bankruptcy under Chapter 13, which is explained in another part of this Money Guide – except here you avoid lawyer fees and the stigma associated with declaring bankruptcy!*

# TABLE TWO

| Name | Percentage Owed | Monthly Payment |
|---|---|---|
| 1. Car payment | 33% | $275 |
| 2. Holt's Furniture | 17% | 142 |
| 3. Auto Credit | 10% | 83 |
| 4. Electrical Appliance | 7% | 58 |
| 5. Small Loans, Inc. | 10% | 83 |
| 6. Federal Bank | 20% | 167 |
| 7. John's Dept. Store | <u>3%</u> | <u>25</u> |
|  | **100%** | **$833** |

**NOTE:** *In figuring our dollar amounts to pay each creditor in Table Two, we used the $833 figure the Formula indicated we can afford instead of the $930 figure that Table One revealed we owe all creditor's monthly.*

**Now use your salesmanship and call or visit all your creditors and sell them the idea of lowering your**

payments to comply with the Formula. Show them what you owe and what you have done, if that's what it takes. If you do not do this, you will upset the entire plan by dipping into your allowance for living costs – or worse, by tapping into your saving just to pay debts.

## *REMEMBER YOUR ARE YOUR NUMBER ONE CREDITOR!*

## *PAY YOURSELF FIRST!*

If you do not wish to call or visit your creditors, the other solution to your debt problem is to arrange a partial consolidation loan (possibly from home equity) to cover some of your debt, in particular those accounts that carry the highest rates of interest or the highest monthly payments. This loan you will pay off out of the $833 set aside for monthly debt payment, and if done right, you will not have to borrow the entire $30,653. In the example given in TABLE ONE, you would only have to borrow $26,668 from a bank, Savings and Loan, credit union, or private source – just enough to pay off those items marked with an asterisk (*) in Table One. Thus, your payments would be:

## *TABLE THREE*

1. $604 to consolidate partial debts – bank or other lenders
2. $51 to Auto Credit
3. $28 to John's Department Store

**Total: $683**

**NOTE:** *If a loan is impossible maybe a smaller approach can be done. Combine a couple of your accounts into a smaller loan and concentrate on paying the smaller loan off first. A little ingenuity perhaps will turn the tide and then concentrate on paying the smaller loan first, so that you can get within the monthly amount you can pay off.*

This reduces the monthly payment from $833 per month to $683 per month, for a reduction of $150 per month. But don't go and blow that $150. This reduction should be set aside in an emergency fund (in an interest-bearing savings account at your bank or other financial institution) for emergencies or unexpected high capital outlays, such as major appliance or automobile breakdowns or replacements. It is important that you establish this emergency fund, as it is estimated that the average credit user has to take out a new loan on the average of once every three years. If you use this emergency fund to dip into when you have an emergency, you could avoid some of the damage done by taking new loans. Plus, when Auto Credit and John's Department Store accounts are paid off, you can then pay more on the consolidation loan and pay it off faster (or add the amount to your emergency fund).

# *THE MECHANICS OF BUDGETING*

As for the mechanics of maintaining a budget, there are various budget systems and approaches that could be used.

One is to use one checking account at your bank or other financial institution to pay the amount for your "fixed" and "temporary" expenses only (remember, these are debt obligations). When your paycheck comes, deposit *only* the amount needed to cover those debts.

How much is that? Use a sheet of paper (or one of our Forms) to keep a running balance of each "fixed" expense and of each "temporary" expense. Subtract this sum from your running balance for that category. In this way, you can know where you stand at all times as far as the balance in each category is concerned, and you will always know whether you are over or under the amount you should have in that category. Of course, you could draw from any account that looks as if it has too much in it, and use those funds to pay for an account that is short the necessary funds to make the full payment that month . . . but you wouldn't' want to do that to often.

To keep things simple with your categories, keep your figures rounded off in whole dollars amounts (as we have already suggested), and where you have a cent amount, put the cent amount in the "Misc." category.

You may also want to use envelopes to keep track of the bills you pay in cash. Obtain a packet of envelopes designed for this purpose and write on each envelope the name of the category. Each payday, put the sum of money designated for this category in your budget envelope. Of course, with this system you would probably accumulate too much cash, which would not be safe to keep around the house, unless it's a category that you would be emptying each month, as, say, for food.

It may take a little work to gather this information, but it is well worth the effort. Keeping track of your finances in this way makes budgeting fun and easy to operate, once it is set up. This is true especially as you see your savings mount month after moth and balances being paid down on those debt accounts.

**NOTE:** *To those who get paid every two weeks: Twice a year or every six months you will realize a three-payment month. This results in your realizing a little extra cash for that 'something extra' you may want to splurge on, or you could use it to get that 'special something' you've been waiting to get, but have been putting off getting. Or you may want to build up some of your budget categories that you have dipped into and which are dangerously low even overdrawn, using your checking account or envelope system.*

# *IMPULSE BUYING IS THE ENEMY!*

**Remember! Curb impulse buying**! Ask yourself, "Do I really need this item?" Put it on a thirty-day waiting list, and at the end of the thirty days, look at it again and see if it is still wanted or has now dropped in priority.

**What is your Net Worth?** If you are the kind of person who is intrigued by the intricacies of finance, then you might want to give yourself a further financial check-up in order to determine your Net Worth. Net Worth is the total value of all your possessions, minus the amount of all your liabilities (debts). This will be discussed in the next section on Forms.

# CHAPTER SEVEN

## *BANKRUPTCY*

Let's say all efforts and plans to bail yourself out of financial difficulty fail (those of you who are not in this predicament can skip this chapter). What do you do now?

If you are in particularly bad financial shape and you have assets that can be converted into cash, you might want to consider selling some of your assets. An expensive car or home may not be necessary; a second car may not be essential; it may be that the large commitment such an item entails can be the very thing that is at the heart of your financial problem.

After the final analysis, however, you may decide that you have now cut back to the bone and that there is no more fat to trim. You can not work out a debt re-organization plan with your creditors for a reduced monthly payment, and no consolidation loan is available.

The only option left seems to be bankruptcy.

If so, there are several types of bankruptcy, and each has different eligibility criteria. Most people will file either Chapter 7 or Chapter 13 Bankruptcy. Chapter 7 is known as **"*straight bankruptcy.*"** In this type of bankruptcy, assets having significant value may be liquidated to pay off debt. Any remaining debt is discharged, and will not have to be paid. If the court feels you are able to pay $10,000 after expenses over the next five years, any Chapter 7 petition will likely be denied. Chapter 13 Bankruptcy is known as **"*debt adjustment.*"** Chapter 13 Bankruptcy allows you to keep some of your assets by creating a 3- to 5-year debt repayment plan. *(There is also a Chapter 11 bankruptcy, meant primarily for businesses. It is commonly used for restructuring. Borders, the national bookstore chain, recently entered Chapter 11 bankruptcy. They are closing some of their stores but keeping the profitable ones open.)*

In some states like Pennsylvania, individuals who want to file for bankruptcy need to participate in credit counseling at some time during the six months preceding the filing. This allows a professional to examine your finances and help determine if this is the best avenue to pursue. If it is, a bankruptcy Petition in the district where you have lived for the past six months is then filed. Along with the petition, many schedules need to be filed. These schedules are quite detailed, and will include information about your income, expenses, debts, assets, taxes and any property you own that may be exempt from liquidation during the bankruptcy process.

After the bankruptcy petition is filed, the court then schedules a meeting of the creditors. The creditors may choose to attend the meeting or not. To conclude the bankruptcy, a financial management course needs to be completed. Of course there are also filing fees, legal fees to the lawyer who files the bankruptcy petition, a trustee's fee, etc. Since each state's laws vary on this matter of bankruptcy, anyone contemplating going down this path should check it all out with any attorney who is knowledgeable in this area of law.

If you successfully complete your plan, it definitely will be considered a *"plus"* on your credit rating. Nevertheless, and regardless of what anyone tells you to the contrary, bankruptcy records will dog your footsteps for years to come. Remember, for whatever reason, the general attitude towards bankruptcy is negative, and you may find it very difficult to live with. Bankruptcy is the blackest possible mark on a credit rating, so carefully consider whether or not your want to go down this road.

If you file for bankruptcy, you will need to do a Net Worth (Assets minus Liabilities).

# CHAPTER EIGHT

## *BUDGET FORMS*

On the following pages, you will find forms that can help you with the following challenges:

1. Income – All Sources
2. Monthly "Fixed" Expenses – Inflexible
3. Monthly "Fixed" Expenses – Flexible
4. Monthly "temporary" debt/expenses – creditors and credit obligations
5. Record of Savings Net worth – Assets minus Liabilities equal Net Worth
6. Net worth – Assets minus Liabilities equal Net Worth
7. Monthly Disbursement Schedule

Name: _____

| INCOME -- ALL SOURCES | BI-WEEKLY | | MONTHLY |
|---|---|---|---|
| | 1st Pay | 2nd Pay | TOTAL |
| | Amount | Amount | |
| Take-Home Pay -- Regular Job | $ | $ | $ |
| Income from Extra Job | | | |
| Take-Home Pay -- Wife's Job | | | |
| Income -- Others in Family | | | |
| Other Income | | | |
| TOTAL -- INCOME ALL SOURCES | | | |
| DEDUCTIONS FROM PAY | HUSBAND | WIFE | TOTAL |
| Federal Income Tax | | | |
| State Tax | | | |
| Earned Income Tax -- Local | | | |
| Pension | | | |
| Hospitalization | | | |
| Group Insurance | | | |
| Savings Bonds | | | |
| Credit Union -- Savings | | | |
| Credit Union -- Loans | | | |
| Stock Options | | | |
| Union Dues | | | |
| Christmas Club | | | |
| Other | | | |
| Other | | | |
| TOTAL DEDUCTIONS | | | |
| TOTAL INCOME LESS TOTAL DEDUCTIONS | | | |

Name: _____

| FIXED EXPENSES - INFLEXIBLE | BI-WEEKLY | | |
|---|---|---|---|
| LIVING EXPENSES | 1st Pay | 2nd Pay | TOTAL |
| Charity | | | |
| Savings & Investments | | | |
| Mortgage or Rent | | | |
| Property Insurance | | | |
| Property Taxes | | | |
| Life Insurance | | | |
| Health-Accident/Hospitalization Insurance | | | |
| Car Insurance | | | |
| Other Insurance (School, Camper, Boat, Summer House) | | | |
| Other Taxes (Excise, Land, School, Personal Property) | | | |
| Electric and Gas | | | |
| Telephone | | | |
| Eat | | | |
| Food (including lunches) | | | |
| Clothing | | | |
| Transportation (Gas & Oil, Car Repairs, Maintenance Costs, License, Registration) | | | |
| Sewer & Water | | | |
| Club & Other Dues | | | |
| Garbage & Trash Collections | | | |
| Other (Baby Sitting, Alimony and/or Child Support, etc.) | | | |
| | | | |
| TOTAL FIXED EXPENSES - INFLEXIBLE | | | |

Name: _____

| FIXED EXPENSES - FLEXIBLE | BI-WEEKLY | | |
|---|---|---|---|
| LIVING EXPENSES | 1st Pay | 2nd Pay | TOTAL |
| Doctor & Dentist; Medical & Drug Bills | | | |
| Cleaning & Laundry | | | |
| Beauty Shop & Hair Cuts | | | |
| Smokes; Hobbies; Beer; Liquor; Sports | | | |
| Babysitting | | | |
| Entertainment - Restaurant | | | |
| Home Improvements; Maintenances | | | |
| Toiletries & Cosmetics | | | |
| Pet Food & Veterinary | | | |
| Vacations | | | |
| Subscriptions (Magazines, Books; Tapes, etc.) | | | |
| Newspapers | | | |
| Home Furnishings | | | |
| Allowances | | | |
| Gifts (Wedding, Birthdays, etc.) | | | |
| Education (Music Lessons, Dancing Lessons, Ski, Tennis, Golf, Courses of Study) | | | |
| Other (Baby Sitting, Alimony and/or Child Support, etc.) | | | |
| TOTAL FIXED EXPENSES - FLEXIBLE | | | |

Name: _____

## TEMPORARY EXPENSES - CREDITORS & CREDIT OBLIGATIONS

| No. | Creditor & Address | Monthly Payment | Date Due | Interest Rate | Upaid Balance | Proposed Payment |
|---|---|---|---|---|---|---|
|  |  |  |  |  |  |  |
|  |  |  |  |  |  |  |
|  |  |  |  |  |  |  |
|  |  |  |  |  |  |  |
|  |  |  |  |  |  |  |
|  |  |  |  |  |  |  |
|  |  |  |  |  |  |  |
|  |  |  |  |  |  |  |
|  |  |  |  |  |  |  |
|  |  |  |  |  |  |  |
|  |  |  |  |  |  |  |
|  |  |  |  |  |  |  |
|  |  |  |  |  |  |  |
|  |  |  |  |  |  |  |
|  |  |  |  |  |  |  |
|  |  |  |  |  |  |  |
|  |  |  |  |  |  |  |
|  |  |  |  |  |  |  |
|  |  |  |  |  |  |  |
| TOTAL |  |  |  |  |  |  |
| TOTAL INDEBTEDNESS |  |  |  |  |  |  |

Name: _____

| Pay Day | SAVINGS | | Pay Day | SAVINGS | |
|---|---|---|---|---|---|
| | Deposits | Total | | Deposits | Total |
| 1 | | | 14 | | |
| 2 | | | 15 | | |
| 3 | | | 16 | | |
| 4 | | | 17 | | |
| 5 | | | 18 | | |
| 6 | | | 19 | | |
| 7 | | | 20 | | |
| 8 | | | 21 | | |
| 9 | | | 22 | | |
| 10 | | | 23 | | |
| 11 | | | 24 | | |
| 12 | | | 25 | | |
| 13 | | | 26 | | |

# *NOTES ON KEEPING TRACK OF YOUR NET WORTH:*

Keeping track of your Net Worth" on a yearly basis is more than fun and games. There are some very real benefits to be realized:

1. Annual "Net Worth" calculation gives you a clear picture of your financial situation. Without this information, it is hard to decide where you stand financially.

2. It helps you in Estate Planning.

    ❖ Is your Life Insurance coverage adequate?

    ❖ Should you have your will rewritten because your financial picture has changed significantly in recent years?

3. Are you saving as much as you could or should?

4. Set up a folder for your "Net Worth" computation. Then put it in a safe place where you know you will be able to find it. This way you can go back each year and see how you calculated it in the past and also compare your new "Net Worth" figure with the previous years.

Name: _____
## NET WORTH - PERSONL FINANCIAL STATEMENT

### ASSETS
Cash in Banks
Savings & Loan Shares
Earnest Money Deposited
Investments: Bonds & Stocks
Investment in Own Business
Accounts and Notes Receivable
Real Estate Owned - Value
Automobiles
Personal Property & Furniture
Life Insurance ($         ) Cash Surrender Value
Other Assets - Itemize

**TOTAL ASSETS**

### LIABILITIES
Notes Payable:
  To Banks
  To Relatives
  To Other
Installment Accounts Payable:
  Automobile
  Other
Other Accounts Payable
Mortgages Payable - Real Estate
Unpaid Real Estate Taxes
Unpaid Income Taxes
Chattel Mortgages
Loans of Life Insurance Policies
  (Include Premiums Advanced)
Other debts - Itemize

**TOTAL LIABILITIES**

**Net Worth - Total Assets Less Total Liabilities**

**TOTAL LIABILITIES & NET WORTH**

Name: _____

**PROPOSED DISBURSEMENT SCHEDULE**

| MONTHS: | 1 | 2 | 3 | 4 | 5 | 6 | 7 | 8 | 9 | 10 | 11 | 12 |
|---|---|---|---|---|---|---|---|---|---|---|---|---|
| Take-Home Pay | | | | | | | | | | | | |
| Savings (10%) | | | | | | | | | | | | |
| Fixed Expenses (70%) | | | | | | | | | | | | |
| Temporary Expenses (20%) | | | | | | | | | | | | |

# *BIBLIOGRAPHY*

Dan Brown II, Shroud Booklet, 1972, p. 3.

Irving Fisher, *The Purchasing Power of Money* (New York, 1920), pp. 31-32.

Benjamin M. Andrews, Jr., *The Value of Money*, (New York, 1926), p. 153.

Paul A. Samuelson, *Economics, Fifth Edition*, McGraw Hill Book Company, Inc. New York, New York, 1961, p. 51.

Gary North, *An Introduction to Christian Economics.* The Craig Press, Nutley, New Jersey, 1976.

David Wiedemer, Robert Wiedemer, Cindy Spitzer. *Aftershock: Protect Yourself and Profit in the Next Global Financial Meltdown*, Wiley & Sons, 2009.

Martin J. McDaniel and Dr. Joseph M. Meyer, Jr. *Don't Bank on It!*, Warner, 1975

Dan Brown II, *The Dawn of a New Age for Mankind Through This Economic Association*

Suarez, Benjamin, *7 Steps to Freedom*. The Publishing Corporation of America, Inc. Canton, Ohio, 1978.

Clason, George S., *The Richest Man in Babylon Booklet*. Hawthorn Books, Inc., New York, New York. 1955-1958, Prentice-Hall, Inc. Englewood Cliffs, New Jersey.

Ferdinand Luneberg, *The Rich and the Super Rich*.

*The Trading Report, September 4, 2011.*

# ABOUT THE AUTHOR

Robert worked in a Management Level Position with the City of Lebanon, PA, Public Works Department for 25 years.

Robert operated his own business, Kline & Sons, Inc., Financial Consultants, in Lebanon, PA for a number of years.

He did Financial Counseling with the late Larry Burkett Ministry, Christian Financial Concepts, for several years.

Robert took a business course with the Wharton School of Business, University of Pennsylvania, Philadelphia, PA.

He was a Registered Representative with Waddell & Reed, Inc., Financial Advisors, [stockbrokers for United Funds-a Billion Dollar Industry] working out of their Harrisburg, PA, Office.

Robert is an Alumnus of the Philadelphia Biblical University, Langhorne, PA.

He is a veteran of World War II, having served in the United States Navy.

He resides with his wife, Mary, in the Lebanon, PA, area.